To You,
From Him

Love notes from God

Love

♡

TeQuila Connors

TO YOU FROM HIM

Unless otherwise noted, all scripture quotations are taken from The Holy Bible, New International Version.

Books may be purchased by contacting the author at authorprenuer@mail.com or http://authorprenuer.net.

ISBN 978-1-942844-21-1

Prov31 Publishing (authorprenuer.net)
Printed in USA

Dedication

To, You

These letters were written to help you understand the love that God has for you. You have to know that no matter your situation, He loves you. It is possible to feel he no longer loves you or that He never loved you at all. This is not true. He loves you more than you can ever imagine and He will always.

Preface

This book was inspired by my favorite scripture, 3 John 2. Every time I read this scripture, I think of it as a love note written especially for me from the Lord. In *To You, From Him* it is my prayer to speak to the hearts of many through the word of God. This collection is revelation of what our Father is saying to us in various scriptures of the Bible. *To You, From Him* forms the conversation of love between the reader and our Heavenly Father. These letters can be a source of meditation and give a greater understanding of God's word as it is applied to the readers' life.

All scriptures are inspired by the Holy Spirit and compiled into the Holy Bible for our admonishment as well as encouragement. Through this life, we will face experiences that will try to take us down and we need to know that there is comfort in the Word of God. We need to know that we can find peace that goes beyond our normal reasoning, joy that will strengthen us when we have no natural strength left, and new life when all seems dead around us. We receive all of these things when we know and trust that our Heavenly Father gives them freely without condition. We have all we need in His words.

• • • • • •

Heavenly Father,

The trajectories of life tend to make me forget who I am; that I am loved, that you will never leave me, that many are my afflictions but you deliver me from them all.

In your word, I remember that I am the righteousness of You. I remember that I am fearfully and wonderfully made. I remember that I am made in your image and likeness. This means I have an imagination that will remove me from this life in my flesh and take me to a world created for me by you.

In your word, my memory is restored. In your word, I remember that I am not my possessions, I am not my social status, I am not my environment, and I am not who "they" say I am. I am who you, Heavenly Father say that I am. I am all that and much, much more.

In your Word, I remember that I am Yours and You are mine!

Amen

Table of Contents

Introduction of Author

TeQuila Connors is a native of Hopewell, VA. She is an entrepreneur, dancer, and published author.

TeQuila enjoys reading and has become a creative poet and intuitive writer over the last two decades. She has just in recent years decided to transform her writings into books. Other works by TeQuila are **"Love Is Air: poems of my journey" and "After Your Morning After: spiritual growth from inside out".**

While studying the word of God one day sparked a feeling of such love. This love, she knew came directly from God and jumped right off of the pages. This encounter inspired TeQuila to put on paper all the love she received. She knew that the Holy Spirit does not give us revelation for just ourselves. She knew this love needed to be shared. Get to know Him for yourself in these pages. You will swoon over how much He loves you.

I Am
(Person of God)

~

Our Heavenly Father is everything to us. He takes on the form of anything we may need at a specific time in our life and fills the space between the promise and possession.

Jehovah Jireh

Beloved,

As I was with your brother Abraham, I will be with you. There is nothing I will withhold from you because you trust Me, just as he did. Whatever the plan, I will provide what you need to fulfill it. There can be some obstacles along your journey. I will make a way of escape for you. You will be able to go over the obstacle, go under it, or go around it but you will succeed.

At times, you will be uncertain that you are equipped to finish what has been started. You may even feel confused. You can count on me to make sure you have all you need to accomplish your goals. There is nothing too hard for Me and there is nothing you cannot do because we are together.

Your Provider

"Abraham looked up and there in a thicket he saw a ram caught by its horns. He went over and took the ram and sacrificed it as a burnt offering instead of his son. So Abraham called that place the Lord will provide. And to this day it is said, "On the mountain of the Lord it will be provided." Genesis 22:13-14

Jehovah Nissi

Beloved,

The world is against you. Everything in it is part of the enemy's plans for you to fail. Each day is full of troubles and trials. Go ahead; shake your head in disgust. Nevertheless, the banner that I have set around you will protect you. You will win every battle without having to fight them yourself. Just stand behind the banner and watch your foes as they fall to the ground.

You have even won battles that you did not know you were involved. People smile in your face but curse you to your back. I hear them. Just as I bless those that bless you, they will be cursed for cursing you. Some would dare to plot schemes against you. They plan situations to trap you or hurt you. Pray for them, they know not what they do. They will fall into the trap themselves. Victory has been and will always be ours.

Your Banner

"Moses built an altar and named it "God My Banner"
Exodus 17:15 (MSG)

Jehovah Rophe

Beloved,

Does a cough mean pneumonia? Does a sneeze mean the flu? Does a headache mean an aneurism? No. I took on all sickness and disease so that they would be nailed to the cross. I sacrificed my son so that you will not have to suffer from them. Do not allow symptoms to become your situation. Just because things are thrown your way does not mean you have to catch them. Your body is designed to reject anything that I did not place in it. Therefore, the symptoms you experience are just the results of your body rejecting what I did not put there. Do the same in your mind and spirit, My Love. Reject what gives you dis-ease. Walk in your healed state, walk in your healing.

Your Healer

"LORD my God, I called to you for help, and you healed me." Psalm 30:2

Jehovah Mekaddishkem

Beloved,

Do you remember the game, *"Follow the Leader"*? It is a simple game but has such a profound lesson. How well you pay attention to the leader determines whether you are left standing. Follow my lead of sanctification. Allow my journey to be your journey. Learn from what you have seen in me. This will ensure that you will be where I am someday. I have created the pattern of purification. All you need to do is follow that template and you will be purified, holy, and blessed. Follow my lead.

Your Sanctifier

"For them I sanctify myself, that they too may be truly sanctified." John 17:19

Jehovah Rohi

Beloved,

You want this? You got it. You need that? You got it. As we travel this journey together, you will have everything you need. There will be no lack in your life. Every need in your household is met. There is nothing missing. Nothing will be broken. You will live in abundance so that you can wear the best, eat the best, live beyond your imagination, and be a blessing to those around you. Just ask me and it is yours. I take care of my own.

Your Shepard

"The LORD is my shepherd, I lack nothing."
Psalm 23:1

Jehovah Tsidkenu

Beloved,

My love for you is so great. In fact, "great" is an understatement. There is not a word in creation to describe my love for you. I want you to know what it means to be truly saved. Therefore, I have become your savior. I have redeemed you from curses. I have delivered you from the tricks of the enemy. I have blessed the works of your hands and caused you to prosper in your diligence. This is what a savior does, My Love. Anything that can possibly bring you harm or defeat, I have stopped in its tracks.

Your Savior

"In his days Judah will be saved and Israel will live in safety. This is the name by which he will be called: The Lord our Righteous Savior." Jeremiah 23:6

Jehovah Shalom

Beloved,

Many things have been on your mind lately. You wonder if I am with you when you are sad and lonely. You wonder if I care when you are hurt. You wonder if I am listening when you call my name. You do not have to wonder, I will never leave you.

You are afraid when you are in an unfamiliar place in your life. You are afraid when asked to try something new. You are afraid to trust a stranger with things that are dear to you. You are afraid to forgive when you have been wronged. You do not have to be afraid, peace I give you.

Peace and blessings are my intentions for you. The peace I give you will elevate you above any situation or circumstance. If you cannot move because of how you feel, I will move on your behalf. You may be catching hell on every turn but my peace will allow you to remain calm, My Love. Others will look on you and gasp, "Why aren't you freaking out?" You can say with complete confidence that I have you. Be at peace and be still. Nothing is as bad as it seems. My comfort will keep you.

Your Peace

"I have told you all this so that you may have peace in me. Here on earth you will have many trials and sorrows. But take heart, because I have overcome the world." John 16:32-33 (NLT)

Jehovah Hoseenu

Beloved,

From the start I envisioned you in my mind. I wanted to be able to connect with another that is like me in many ways. Therefore, I made you. I made you in my image and in my likeness. I formed a body for your spirit to reside here on Earth. I created you so that not only will you be beautiful on the inside but also on the outside. I put systems in your body that flow exactly like the heavens. I formed you in such a way that if anything tries to enter your body that I did not place in it, your body would reject it. I have given you a mind with a balance of imagination, intellect, will and emotions. I created you to have the ability to operate not only in the spirit realm but also in the natural. I made you like me. Cherish our similarities. I do.

Your Maker

"Come, let us bow down in worship, let us kneel before the LORD our Maker." Psalms 95:6

Jehovah Shammah

Beloved,

I know the noise of this life gets louder than my voice at times. This noise can be in the form of media scares, bill collectors, family and friend worries, personal thoughts. It can be unbearable to you, I know. The enemy can also shoot fiery darts your way and when things seem lost, he will kick you while you are down. All the while, I am with you. I am with you in fear. I am with you in sorrow. I am with you when you worry. I am with you when you are in pain. I am with you always. Not only am I with you, I will carry you through these trials. I destroy what tries to destroy you. Notice that I said, "try" because nothing that comes near you will defeat you. I am with you, My Love.

Always,

"Only do not rebel against the LORD. And do not be afraid of the people of the land, because we will devour them. Their protection is gone, but the LORD is with us. Do not be afraid of them." Numbers 14:9

Yours
(Promises of God)

~

It is blessed that the responses of our God are always "Yes" and "Amen". He promises many things and He is not a man, He cannot lie. So trust that He who promised is willing and more than able to perform it.

Redemption

Beloved,

I hope you do not believe that because of your past mistakes, that I am not with you any longer. I hope you do not believe that I will not forgive you for what you have done. Please do not feel this way. My son's blood has redemptive power. His blood has redeemed you from what you have done long before it happened. Through this same shed blood, you have been forgiven for your sins. Please believe this. If you believe and come to me for my forgiveness, you can have it. My forgiveness is yours if you want it. I am waiting to show you that I have already given it to you. You just have to accept it. So go easy on yourself, you are redeemed.

Your Redeemer

"In him we have redemption through his blood, the forgiveness of sins, in accordance with the riches of God's grace..." Ephesians 1:7

Redemption

Beloved,

No matter what you face today or tomorrow, know that I am always with you. When you laugh, I laugh. When you cry, I cry. When you are rejoicing, I rejoice with you. When a dark cloud hovers over you, I will encourage you to continue to let your light shine.

When you are doing what you know is wrong, I will still be with you. If you ever leave me, I will wait for you to come back to me. There is nothing or no one that can turn me away from loving you. Not even you. You have accepted the gift I sent you, so there is no turning back. There is no separating us from now on.

Yours truly,

"For I am persuaded that neither death nor life, nor angels nor principalities nor powers, nor things present nor things to come, nor height nor depth, nor any other created thing, shall be able to separate us from the love of God which is in Christ Jesus our Lord." Romans 8:38-39 (NKJV)

Redemption

Beloved,

Laws have been put into place to keep order and peace. Some older laws were man made and were impossible to keep. According to the old law, punishment is death for not following the law to the letter. Trying to follow the law can place you under a curse. I know you are not perfect. I know that it is difficult to keep the entire law. So I have a remedy- My Son. My son has taken on all sins according to the law and he died in your place. You have been redeemed by his death on the cross. This does not give you permission to break the law but you have been granted the opportunity for a fair trial and not immediate death.

Yours truly,

"Christ redeemed us from the curse of the law by becoming a curse for us, for it is written: "Cursed is everyone who is hung on a pole." Galatians 3:13

Reassurance

Beloved,

It is my wish always for you to be healthy. Not only physical health but mental and spiritual health as well. I will provide for you a balanced diet of spiritual food and physical food, daily. I will watch you while you sleep so peacefully each night. When you awake in the morning, I will hand you all the goodness and mercy you need throughout your day so you lack nothing.

I cherish you, My Love. I will always root for your prosperity and pleasure until you depart this natural realm and return home to me.

Love,

"Beloved, I pray that you may prosper in all things and be in health, just as your soul prospers."
3 John 1:2 (NKJV)

Reassurance

Beloved,

I saw it when the "snatch back man" towed your car in the middle of the night and you had to catch the bus to work in the morning. I saw when your best friend stabbed you in the back over money. I saw when the one you loved left you for another. I saw when the doctor diagnosed you with cancer and said that he did not know what to do for you.

I know you would rather none of these things happen to you. Don't fret. Just let me know what you want me to do and I will do it. All that was taken will be returned to you in double. All that was broken will be replaced with a higher quality model. All that the doctor says I will make it right. Peace I write to you because I have overcome this world and all that it may throw your way.

Yours truly,

"Do not be anxious about anything, but in every situation, by prayer and petition, with thanksgiving, present your requests to God. And the peace of God, which transcends all understanding, will guard your hearts and your minds in Christ Jesus." Philippians 4:6-8

Reassurance

Beloved,

Something has come up. Something is always coming up. "When it rains it pours", right? Rejoice in these times. I have faith that your faith is strong enough to handle it all. In these times, your faith is being tested. I have your "A" waiting for you. I know you will pass the test. Believe in you, because I do.

With Love,

"Consider it a sheer gift, friends, when tests and challenges come at you from all sides. You know that under pressure, your faith-life is forced into the open and shows its true colors. So don't try to get out of anything prematurely. Let it do its work so you become mature and well-developed, not deficient in any way." James 1:2-4 (MSG)

Reassurance

Beloved,

There is no such thing as "woe is me". Those words are not for you. Your life is part of my plan and my plan is final. The good thing about being with me is that everything that comes your way or is taken away are all part of my plan. I planned the beginning, middle, and end of your story. The beginning. Good. The middle? Good. The end? Good. My word gives you a glimpse of my divine plan. Continue to follow my plan and as you go, look to your future. Your future looks much better than things look right now. If you are preoccupied with the future I have for you, todays worries will not have a major impact on you.

Yours truly,

"I know what I'm doing. I have it all planned out – plans to take care of you, not abandon you, plans to give you the future you hope for." Jeremiah 29:11(MSG)

Reassurance

Beloved,

Yes, it does seem like you have been singled out. Yes, it does seem like you have a bull's-eye on your back. Yes, at times it seems like you are being picked on by the enemy. But…No, I will not let you be alone in your time of need. No, I will not leave you to go through without a comforter. No, you will not be taken out. Whatever happens to you are the same things that happen to your brothers and sisters because you are set apart. You are my children and tests and trials will come to prove just that. Your lives have been written in a book. The pages turn and life throws things your way. Keep in mind that you are not alone and you will be carried through. So, no matter what page you are on…I got you!

Forever with you,

"No test or temptation that comes your way is beyond the course of what others have had to face. All you need to remember is that God will never let you down; he'll never let you be pushed past your limit; he'll always be there to help you come through it." 1 Corinthians 10:13

Reassurance

Beloved,

I know you love me. I know that whatever I say, you will hide in your heart as a treasure. My teachings, you will pass down to your children so that the generations after you will live in my love as you do. What I have promised to your ancestors are your promises as well. My love for you cannot be moved, cannot be erased, and will not be altered. We share a bond that flows like the ocean. The tides may come in and they go back out but the ocean remains, just like our love. Faithful I will remain to you and even to your children's children. I promise.

Forever Faithful,

"Know therefore that the LORD *your God is God; he is the faithful God, keeping his covenant of love to a thousand generations of those who love him and keep his commandments." Deuteronomy 7:9*

Reassurance

Beloved,

    With me, Faith goes a long way. Unfortunately, we cannot communicate without you having faith. Without faith, things can be very difficult for you to achieve. Things may even be impossible for you. Without faith, you are facing life alone. You may have goals, dreams, aspirations. You may need shelter, clothing, food, and other things you deem are needs. In order to receive any of these you must first have faith. I have given it to you. Faith is your greatest need. With the measure of faith I have given you, the needs that I listed earlier can be met. Exercising your faith makes your faith stronger. With stronger faith, you can believe for greater and it will be granted for you. You can have anything your heart desires. I will never run out. Just work your gift of faith.

Faithfully yours,

"But my God shall supply all your need according to his riches in glory by Christ Jesus."
Philippians 4:19 (KJV)

Reciprocity

Beloved,

Do you know how it feels to want for nothing? Do you know the feeling of being blessed beyond measure? Do you want to know this feeling? Here's what you can do…trust Me. Trust that I will keep my word. Trust that I will do all that I promise. Trust that I have your best interest at heart. Trust that I will overtake you with blessings. All you need to do is return back to me a small portion of what I give to you. Just as your home has bills, my house here on Earth has bills as well. Your tithe will help to pay those bills and to reach those that have not been exposed to the kind of relationship that we have.

Your Financier

"Bring the whole tithe into the storehouse, that there may be food in my house. Test me in this," says the LORD Almighty, "and see if I will not throw open the floodgates of heaven and pour out so much blessing that there will not be room enough to store it." Malachi 3:10-11

Reciprocity

Beloved,

Your choosing to do the right thing compels me to make sure you live your days in prosperity and pleasure. As soon as you find out what it is that I want, you go for it! You are such a blessing to my people. You go above and beyond in your service. I can't stop pouring out praises for your righteousness. You trust that whatever I ask you to do, that it will lead to your success.

Some things that I bring before you can be hard tasks, they may even seem impossible but my grace sustains you. I will never ask of anything to your demise. Whatever it may be, it is only to ensure a life of pleasure for you. I want to see you content in this life. These are my plans for you. Whatever I bring before you, see them through. Prosperity and pleasure is yours for the taking.

Your Contentment

"If they obey and serve him, they will spend the rest of their days in prosperity and their years in contentment." Job 36:11

Reciprocity

Beloved,

Guess what I have for you. Everything! More than you can imagine. I have everything that you see and want. You work so diligently for the kingdom; I have no choice but to give you anything your heart desires. You are consistent in giving of your gifts and your time. You are loving to everyone. You work hard to make sure my vision comes to pass. You seek out how I would handle a situation rather than go on your own judgment. You know the right way to get things done. I am so proud of you and your reward is Everything!

With Love,

"But seek first his kingdom and his righteousness, and all these things will be given to you as well." Matthew 6:33

Reciprocity

Beloved,

You have two hands. When you use one hand to give, you can use the other to receive. This is so that there is a constant flow in your life. Now, how much is given back to you is really up to you. When you give, expect to receive. There will always be time to sow and time to reap. Receiving is "in your hands", literally. The measure you give is the measure you will receive back. When you purpose to give of yourself and of your substance in abundance, abundance is exactly what you will get back. This giving is of the heart. Do not hold back your giving because you don't think you can afford to give. You can't afford *not* to give. I will provide for you if you have the heart to give. Giving opens your hands to receive.

With Love,

"Give and it will be given to you. A good measure, pressed down, shaken together and running over, will be poured into your lap. For with the measure you use, it will be measured to you." Luke 6:38

Reciprocity

Beloved,

I wish that you would be blessed in all your efforts. I wish that you would be blessed in all you do. Life can go much smoother if you follow the rules. Not just the rules of the world but also my law. This perfect law works on your behalf as well. My law keeps you free from worrying about what the world tries to do to you. My law keeps you free from the enemy's schemes. My law keeps you free from self-inflicted wounds. As you become more intimate with the word, my law is revealed to you. Continuing in this law makes you a better citizen of this world by creating a life of not only freedom but also overflow that you may bless others.

Your Law- maker

"But whoever looks intently into the perfect law that gives freedom, and continues in it—not forgetting what they have heard, but doing it—they will be blessed in what they do."   *James 1:25*

Reciprocity

Beloved,

If you want a larger harvest, just ask. I will supply as much seed you need to create the harvest that you want. The farmer does not obtain a harvest that will provide for his family and for others by planting a handful of seeds. You want a large harvest; you have to sow a large seed. Since, everything in the Earth is mine. There is never a shortage. As long as you sow, I will increase your seeds as well as your harvest. How, you ask. I have people in place waiting to connect with you, to give to you on my behalf. These people have the necessary resources to get you to the seeds.

Love,

"Now he who supplies seed to the sower and bread for food will also supply and increase your store of seed and will enlarge the harvest of your righteousness." 2 Corinthians 9:10

Rest

Beloved,

Unexpected obstacles can be difficult I know. From the loss of your job and car. To when you were evicted from your home. To add salt to insult, your fiancé decided not to appear for your wedding day. During this time of tribulation, I cried with you, My Heart. I never want to see you in pain. It may seem like all is lost but you have all to gain. I allowed these things to happen because I see such greatness in you. These setbacks were just for you to appreciate what I have prepared for you even more. Nothing that hurts you is to your demise because I have a plan.

All that has been taken will be returned to you one hundred fold. These tests have become your testimony. You not only will recover what has been taken, you will be able to share this testimony and deliver someone else.

Love,

"Many are the afflictions of the righteous: but the Lord delivereth him out of them all."
Psalm 34:19 (KJV)

Rest

Beloved,

Take a deep breath. Take another deep breath. Look in front of you. Look on both sides of you. Look behind you. There is nothing there. There is nothing left to hurt you. There is no one there. There is no one there to hurt you any longer.

Lie back and kick up your feet. Clasp your hands behind your head and close your eyes. Rest, My Love. Rest from troubles, worries, and fears. Rest in my arms. I have taken everything and everyone away that could destroy you.

Your Rest

"But now the LORD *my God has given me rest on every side, and there is no adversary or disaster."*
1 Kings 5:3-5

Rest

Beloved,

My arms are wide open. Come to Daddy and tell me all about it. Use my chest for your head to rest on. Use my shoulder to lean on. Use my sleeve to wipe your tears. I will listen. I will keep your secrets. I will quietly caress your back while you let it all out. Just let it out.

You are being treated unfairly by others. You are persecuted for doing what is right. You lost someone you love. You cannot seem to get a break. Your money is short. You are not thinking clearly. Whatever it is, I can take it. I will take it. I will take it all away.

Your Comfort

"Come to me, all you who are weary and burdened, and I will give you rest." Matthew 11:28

Rest

Beloved,

What I have given you in my word will be your shield. My plan is fool proof and you can depend on me always. Remember that you are a spiritual being and your spirit will always be connected to mine. Living a natural life can be complicated at times but I am here. My spirit resides with you. My spirit is in you. So be free, My Love. Be free to smile. Be free to sing. Be free to dance. Be free to live a spirit-filled life.

Love Always,

"Now the Lord is the Spirit, and where the Spirit of the Lord is, there is freedom."
2 Corinthians 3:17

You Are Mine
(Precious to God)

~

It brings about a warm feeling inside to know that you are loved. Gods loves us and has loved us even before we even existed. He goes to great lengths proving to us that we are precious to Him.

Original

Beloved,

You are my most prized creation. You are so much like me. I know because I made you that way. I have created you to be *you* and no one else. You are perfect to me. You are perfect just the way you are. There is no one like you.

I love you for accepting how I created you. I love that you look in the mirror and smile at yourself because you like what you see. I love that you love yourself just as I do.

Your Reflection

"Then God said, "Let us make mankind in our image, in our likeness…" Genesis 1:26

Original

Beloved,

Everything I create is good and not to be rejected by anyone, not even you. There is so much about you that sets you apart from all of my creation. I see so much potential in you. You are doing great things. You will continue to do great things. When I look at you, I smile because you are so beautiful: inside and out.

There is no one with your smile. There is no one with your eyes. There is no one with your personality. There is no one with your heart. You were created with a purpose. Everything about you can be used to attract others to me. You are wonderful. I celebrate your uniqueness. I celebrate you, with you.

With love,

"I praise you because I am fearfully and wonderfully made..." Psalms 139:14

Exclusive

Beloved,

I sacrificed my only son to show you the depth of my love for you. Before you were born, I wanted to make sure when you arrived you had a fighting chance in this corrupt world. I loved you before you even knew for yourself that I existed. Before you came into this world, I made a major sacrifice to ensure a good life for you.

My only son was crucified so you would not have to live in sin. My son was buried so you would not have to die. My son rose from the dead so you would believe he was sent to go through hell on your behalf. Even if you were to die today, you will only die to your natural body. Your spirit will never die and you will forever be mine because you believe.

Affectionately yours,

"For God so loved the world that he gave his one and only Son, that whoever believes in him shall not perish but have eternal life." John 3:16

Exclusive

Beloved,

Although I created everyone, not everyone has me in mind. I am always mindful of you. I am always mindful of everyone. At most times, you feel underserving of my love. I love you always. I love you even when you hurt me by doing what I ask you not to do. I love you before you even think about doing wrong. It is really rare for someone to die for someone else. Especially if they feel, that person is not worth it. My son died for all. I sacrificed my only son for the deserving and the undeserving. Do not let anyone tell you that I do not love you. I did this to show you that I love you. I loved you first and I love you always.

With all my love,

"You see, at just the right time, when we were still powerless, Christ died for the ungodly. Very rarely will anyone die for a righteous person, though for a good person someone might possibly dare to die. But God demonstrates his own love for us in this: While we were still sinners, Christ died for us."
Romans 5:6-8

Unique

Beloved,

You are always on my mind. There is not a second, minute, or hour that I am not thinking of you. I am always thinking of ways to show you how much you are loved. I cannot stop thinking of how proud I am of you. I am always smiling because I am always thinking of you. I think about how my plans and decisions affect you. You are my most cherished. I want you to know that I will never forget about you. I cannot and will not stop thinking of you.

On my mind always,

"What is mankind that you are mindful of them, human beings that you care for them?" Psalm 8:4

Unique

Beloved,

Living this life requires you to stand out from the crowd. You do not have to do what everyone else is doing. Remember when your mother asked you, "If everyone else jumps off a bridge will you?" You may want to do some things that is not beneficial to you. You may want some things that you do not need. Please remember that I *know* what is best for you and that I *want* what is best for you.

Take a chance with me. Come with me on my journey. It may not always be pleasant to your outer self but your inner self will be strengthened to the degree that you can withstand anything. The benefits will far outweigh the persecution of living outside of the crowd.

Yours truly,

"Then Jesus said to his disciples, "Whoever wants to be my disciple must deny themselves and take up their cross and follow me." Matthew 16:24

Distinctive

Beloved,

Do you know how long I have waited for you? I have been waiting for you since I created the Heavens and the Earth. I have been waiting for you since I created humankind. I had this plan, you see. Now that you have accepted my son, my plan can be fulfilled. You are now my child as well and everything I have is yours.

I want you to have everything as a token of my love for you. I want to throw a big party and you will be the guest of honor. I am so full of joy. To make you this happy is my delight. It blesses me to bless you.

Your Father

"How blessed is God! And what a blessing he is! He's the Father of our Master, Jesus Christ, and takes us to the high places of blessing in him. Long before he laid down earth's foundations, he had us in mind, had settled on us as the focus of his love, to be made whole and holy by his love. Long, long ago he decided to adopt us into his family through Jesus Christ. (What pleasure he took in planning this!) He wanted us to enter into the celebration of his lavish gift-giving by the hand of his beloved Son."
Ephesians 1:3-6 MSG

Distinctive

Beloved,

Your choice to follow me has singled you out among your peers. "Who do you think you are?" "Do you think you are better than us?" They may ask you these questions. Your answer is "Yes, I am a new person and Yes, I am better." Everything about you has changed. You are now better than you were before. You may have done what is said about you but you are no longer the person they say you were.

You have a clean slate no matter how much others try to remind you of your past. I know you like new things. It is even better when you yourself are new, refreshed. Take it all in. Lay back and bask in your newness.

Your Refreshing

"Therefore, if anyone is in Christ, the new creation has come: The old has gone, the new is here!" 2 Corinthians 5:17

P.S...

Thank you, Reader for sharing in these love notes from our Heavenly Father. It is my prayer that these words touched your heart and soul. It is important that we know and understand that God always has our best interest in mind. He loves us more than we can imagine and it is evident in His word. Our lives are held together by His grace and His love. These letters are just a few reminders. I challenge you to search the scriptures for in them you will find all of His thoughts about you.

Please feel free to share your thoughts. It would be a blessing to hear from you. Stay blessed.

http://facebook.com/prov31publishing